T0157621

Fear After

Fear After

BEA LITHERLAND

iUniverse, Inc.
New York   Bloomington

Fear After

Copyright © 2009 Bea Litherland

All rights reserved. No part of this book may be used or reproduced by any means, graphic, electronic, or mechanical, including photocopying, recording, taping or by any information storage retrieval system without the written permission of the publisher except in the case of brief quotations embodied in critical articles and reviews.

iUniverse books may be ordered through booksellers or by contacting:

iUniverse
1663 Liberty Drive
Bloomington, IN 47403
www.iuniverse.com
1-800-Authors (1-800-288-4677)

Because of the dynamic nature of the Internet, any Web addresses or links contained in this book may have changed since publication and may no longer be valid. The views expressed in this work are solely those of the author and do not necessarily reflect the views of the publisher, and the publisher hereby disclaims any responsibility for them.

ISBN: 978-1-4401-7079-9 (sc)
ISBN: 978-1-4401-7077-5 (dj)
ISBN: 978-1-4401-7078-2 (ebk)

Library of Congress Control Number: 2009935495

Printed in the United States of America

iUniverse rev. date: 12/15/2009

Foreword

This selection of poetry is intended to take the reader on an emotional roller-coaster journey: from feelings of remembrance and nostalgia downward to regret and despair; then to the bottom—the lowest point—followed by a slow journey up, through a process of hope and acceptance to a state of calm; finally, to a peak where all is visible and the horizon can once more be seen.

Let the journey begin.

Contents

PART ONE: Reminiscence and Nostalgia

Anniversary 3

May 5

Inheritance 6

In Golders Green with Sade 8

The photograph of my son, the policeman 9

Reminiscence about love 10

A New Year resolution confronted with All Saint's Day 11

If it hadn't been for the sound of bats, frogs, and cicadas,
      it would be 13

Today 14

For you 15

Tibetan dream 16

Between arrival and departure 17

The moment 18

PART TWO: From Nostalgia to Despair

No need for a title 23

Time 24

The mirror's reflection 25

Incompetence 26

Badly read 27

There is only one page left 28

Only for a while 29

Apology 30

Much too much about nothing 31

Basic instinct 32

Lost today 33

Going nowhere on the way to somewhere 34

Reflection 35

I am because 36

To my sister 37

Streetwise 38

Being upstairs 39

If I were prettier or younger 40

It could be and it can be 41

Relax 42

Separated 43

Jet lag 44

Blown away 45

PART THREE: From Despair to Hope

As promised 49

Creation 50

Satan's Ball 51

Impression 52

It was a word at the beginning 53

Meaning diversion 54

Carpe Diem 55

Jealousy 56

Letter 57

Rerooted 58

Where do we come back from? 59

The power of fear 60

We 61

On being armed 62

Striving for a poem 63

Fear after 64

PART FOUR: From Hope to Calm

In the rhythm of the waltz. 69

On the beach. 70

Tranquility 71

The Old Devil Sea. 72

Landing in Tibet 73

The colour of China 74

Stranger. 75

Everlasting summer. 76

A drop of adjustment 77

Back to idyll 78

Victoria's frogs. 79

Good luck from Angkor 80

Balcony. 81

The desert garden 82

Justification. 83

Calmness. 84

Tradition. 85

To be born now or later. 86

Dirty hands. 87

I love you my way 88

Part One

Reminiscence and Nostalgia

To be carried on the wings of memory, to the places that no longer belong. To face people whom I left behind, or who left me behind.

The best memories make me feel so sad. The salted tear (I feel happily ashamed) runs down my cheeks, and the longing for something as it was, is left in my memory like a trophy.

Now I see myself in the future missing what I experience at this moment. Then the moment is gone—it was never here. Everything is nostalgia.

Anniversary

It has been three long years
Since you have been dead.
Though dead sounds serious,
I'm sure you would make joke of it—
If it wasn't for you being dead.

The changes that you would never have expected
Happened.
The changes you expected
Haven't happened yet.

On the anniversary of your passing away
I lit a Yazar candle.
It happened in Kuala Lumpur this year.

It felt strange in some strange way
That I carry on alive,
And you carry on being dead.

The continuity of death is persistent,
Accomplished, and firm: it lacks nothing.
It doesn't deal with being too early or too late.
Time and space don't make sense.
In fact continuity is the process,
That death totally erased.

And life (on the contrary) is persistent.
But not accomplished or firm.
Life totally embraces continuity, *adores it.*
And to cherish death?

It seems that life is a happy, bouncy, yellow balloon.
Full of air, and—with the advance of time—
It will deflate and get wrinkled,
And less bouncy.
And when its time comes,

The balloon will expel its last breath.
And then the yellow, happy, once-bouncy balloon,
Will be dead.

May

It doesn't take long now, to realise
That May is not coming
With a bouquet of lilacs
Put into a vase by my mother's hands.

It doesn't bring that great, carefree feeling
Into my constantly perturbed mind,
Though May used to walk with sandals,
Making my heels chilly from the cold ground.

May brought colour to my childhood cheeks,
And a spectacular certainty that I was bound to achieve.

So May! Where are you now?
I would like to store you
For a galactically lasting thought
As the freshness of a counsellor,
Satisfying my lot.

Inheritance

There is not and now won't ever be
The sound of a ringing telephone.

There is a greyness of the misty night,
And holding a nostalgic reality—
The dull light of street lamps.

There is a candle, slowly burning down.
A glass of porter, casting a mysterious shadow
On the faint line of the fridge.

There is also, over there, the place where a bathroom would be,
But instead are old bicycles and jars full of jam.

There is the big brown jar having no meaning today.
And also the smaller milk jar, almost hidden.

But who today might remember the milk,
Which in the past was drunk so the future could grow up?
And even if there is one who remembers,
What effect could it have?

Her old handbag with two fatigued handles, like ears,
Is also lying there.
They try to force from me an answer:
What else is it still possible to do with them?

Sweets and biscuits, biscuits and sweets.
In the old days I was running for them.
So clever and so smart!
But now, today, I am thankful,
Knowing how much more it is possible
To carry on those ears of the old handbag.

Let me enjoy for a little longer

She still exists, still lives here.
In reminiscences she multiplies herself today.
Although passed away quietly, she sits here
On the bench of unfulfilled dreams.

But now she can see more clearly.
Nothing ties anymore her legs.
She sits and again admires
The cheerful smile of a little girl,
Who made herself Queen,
To live in the sand palace.

And later, together in the flat,
By the light of the green and yellow butterflies,
They eat supper by the sound of the cicada
That sings to her hidden children a lullaby.

And later the hanging clock
Will be chiming its ancient song,
Until it brings to life the Mistress
Whose love poured meaning
Into its distinguished tone.

And then only the levelling breath of a little girl remains.
Clock and peace
Are floating to the unknown places of tomorrow
In order to wake up and appreciate their being.

In Golders Green with Sade

I am young!
Walking briskly
In the chilly autumn noon.

Sade smoothly jazzes to my ears.
Life is promising.
I believe
I am young and not a fool.

The sun of Golders Green
Is aptly golden.
A few leaves under my feet
Provide a reminder
That my will is (although it isn't) thoroughly free.

The children, jumping in and out of car seats.
The fish shop, closed on Monday,
The bakers, selling wedding rolls.

Happiness emerging from stability:
A reliable routine?
Not for me. Not yet.

The photograph of my son, the policeman

He came for coffee.

His police radio was making a disturbing noise.
I had the impression
That some heavy arresting was going on inside this box.

I took a photo of him.
It made him feel uptight.
His uniform looks rough, he said,
'And I prefer to look smart.'

Reminiscence about love

How much do I care?
Let us say not too much.
Everything became relative—
As if my life was trying to match some theory.

How much do I say?
Let me think … Much too much;
I give myself away
By being harmlessly detached.

How much courage do I have left?
Let me dream as much as on that dreamy night.
If only love could be like dreams,
And consist only of love.

A New Year resolution confronted with All Saint's Day

I imagined (or rather assumed bravely),
That your New Year resolutions were achieved,
As all dreams used to come true.
At least in a distorted way.

Yours came,
In the highest duty:
Your death.

You had your say.
You had your A and your B.
You proved, and disapproved,
And meant to improve.

And you did!
Reaching for mortality
Infinite reached finite
And the highest justice was done.

***

Life, like the show, must go on,
And All Saint's Day must be respected.

All cemeteries in Poland glow with thousands of candle lights today.
And I, far from home, maintained my tradition.
Alone I was carrying a candle for you.
On the way I crossed the park.

The same place where we used to walk our Doberman, Bruno.
Take toddler Maja to play.
The benches, the rose garden.
The neglected arboretum.

All the same, all the same, all there.
Only the gate leading to your grave was closed.
Due to this being the Holy Day.

I heard you complaining clearly:
'Oh! Silly, silly girl.
You knew the cemetery is closed on the Sabbath Day.
Never mind,' you said.
'It's good you came.'

You didn't say anything about missing or regretting:
Me, world, life, and so on.
I heard you talking.
Lightly, brightly, with enthusiasm.

In a sense it was as if you were a spirit of easiness
Carrying eternity along.

***

Before you went, you said
There won't be any longing or missing *there*.
'I may become your inspiration.'

Perhaps you were right.
It was such a pleasure to take pen and paper today,
And write.

If it hadn't been for the sound of bats, frogs, and cicadas, it would be …

Almost as we were.
The past just a thought away.
Two candles—nostalgia.
I and my shadow.
Will we ever be able to separate?

Today

Under two tall pine trees,
An upset track, within which
Existence ceased.

I cleared the pine needles and dust from the grave.
It brought me closer to love after death,
And longing to the silence that only death can create.

For a little human (who posed a sensible question),
I gave a satisfactory answer.
That you are not under this stone, respectable,
But somewhere above us, outside space,
With anxiously flying angels.

For you

I was waiting for you.
How long you'd never guess.
I was counting the years,
And unmercifully descending
Into less and less.

I imagined your hair,
And the place where we would be together.
I see happiness on your little face.
And a fairy would come to us, making you 'laughadise.'
'What do you mean, fairy?'
I would ask.
But instead of your answer,
Reality materialized.
The monument was raised,
And strength
Has subsided.

Only you
The greatest piece of my dream,
Somehow got frozen and didn't want to exercise
Further laughter with me.

Tibetan dream

Transitory and fleeting.
Just a dream,
Sculpting memory
Into an expanding space,
Into incomprehensible clarity;
Reflecting the chosen, the intriguing, the beautiful and the mystical and—
Most regrettably—
Lack of freedom.

The vivid mind is always willing to play wicked tricks,
Consoling its earthly limitations;
My mind stood still,
Embracing compassion and gratitude.
I stared courageously ahead, and with a deep faith,
Listened to the pacifying silence:
The chanting of Tibetan men.

Between arrival and departure

Between arrival and departure
A short lapse of time
Busily fills the Grail
Grandly called
Being alive.

The contents may vary
But the tempo remains the same
Until the last drop,
Which can't be renamed,
Reaches the edge
And silently, shamelessly,
Time ends.

Departure won't be easy,
But the mystery may be revealed
If there is any mystery to be revealed
Death comes in stages
And doubts may equal sins.
The last smile got frozen.
Tears belong to life.

The moment

The moment is gone.
It was never here.
Ablution in the lily water refreshes,
And the prophets are ready in line,
The tabula rasa is waiting,
And the future will fill the pages,

The moment is here, now
And regretfully,
The stigma of nostalgia
Worships time.

Part Two

From Nostalgia to Despair

As reminiscence makes me search for times lost and inevitably leads to sweetly sad nostalgia, then nostalgia, providing denial and obstruction, can lead to a darkness. Despair.

At a time of deep conviction that my time had zero value; at a time of uncontrollable fear that things could only get worse; at a time when regrets about unchangeable events made my ego go lower and to deeper lows, then the poems became a medium to fight my own feelings.

Regardless of how desperate we might feel, life—our biggest show—must go on, and more so at the time when the dark dame, that unwelcomed intruder, visits us, and leads us into the dark channels of her domain.

Could she have been avoided? Maybe; but she had offered me her hand and I had taken it and had begun to walk with her. She had entered my domain and now walked with me. She would not leave my side until, and if, the next chapter was reached.

No need for a title

It's certainly not restful,
Although it seems to be.
Every fibre of my sensitive tissue
Is crying for self-esteem.

My interior burns,
Casting thousand of sparks,
And every one of them,
Before disappearing,
Has the shape of a human eye.
Deprived of life.

It's not a poem,
And it's not a confession.
Neither protest nor cry—
It's just self-persuasion
That I'm still worth
At least a glance
Through my own eyelash.

Time

If time had been a man,
With wise eyes and nicely curled hair,
I would invite him to waltz.

In rhythm passionately passing nights,
And tasting days full of sense,
I would change for him an hour
Into a timeless and marvellous rest.

And we would dance!
Until the rule of nature raised her hand.
Sentencing him and me to death.

The mirror's reflection

I am telling her
That the most important thing
Is not to be scared.
But she is nevertheless frightened,
Terrified: a fugitive.
She says to herself,
'I am in a bad way.'

Everything new
Has demon's eyes,
A double shade,
Vampire's teeth
Inside—
It wounds, pierces and splits.
Ties with a Gordian knot.
Binds goodness
To disbelief.

Incompetence

Hope and enthusiasm.
I had them: Hope was on the right.
Enthusiasm to my left.
Then they shrank away, disappearing
Inside my sterilized ups and downs.

In retrospect I reflect:
They seasoned me with ephemeral sparks.
But I made such incompetent use of them.
So they lost their brilliance, their charm.

Badly read

An animal living, moving,
changing position,
Inside.

I said (probably stupidly),
'It might be like your friend,'
Though I knew that it sounded wrong,
You said, looking straight ahead,
'My friend!'
With two big black holes,
And at the bottom eyes.
Come here! Will you dare?
Frighten me!
Scare me to the core!
I am the man of brain,
And you?
Pathetic, senseless, pointless,
I just spit at you!
Reproduction of the one human cell
Wrongly reading the code.

There is only one page left

To make this chapter closed,
A few drinks to a present disaster!
And to the future that I still have to carry on.

But the proper toast is to the past,
Just to acknowledge
Its coincidental being.
And the main toast will be to the human bodies
Who sacrifice their unlimited regime.

Only for a while

You must understand
As well as I,
That everything that happened
Is nothing.

Only a traumatic chapter,
With never-ending faith.
Only a strangely designed stage,
With overwhelming demands.

We must be as one.
But live and act apart.

Apology

From the distance you came,
With the quietness and calmness of a cat.

I only wanted to plunge into your calmness.
Instead I stirred its nature.
Therefore it showed us its adverse,
Its beasty and roaring side.

The reverse of meaning—it scared me even more.
In horror I noticed I was pushing you back.
Back into the distance.
And it was the last place I would ever want you to go.

Much too much about nothing

Nothing was told frequently enough
To make nothing believe
That nothing is more of nothing
Than nothing possibly could be.

At the time when nothing wishes
To tidy its nothingness,
Looks in the mirror,
And
The image the mirror brings is me.

Nothing doesn't disappoint.
Expectations are not involved.
Nothing never could and never will
Bear children.
The most nothing can bear
Is a vain hope.

All hopes are shattered
And all dreams are gone.
Nothing creates a universe,
Where hopelessly shed tears go.

So talk gently to nothing.
Nothing might play a sufficient role
In a time where there is no more.

Basic instinct

It would be nice
To put to sleep my inner self

And not even to think that it existed,
As a fibre of sensuous reality.

It would be an achievement
To make the deepest cell of my skin
Not respond to any touch at all.
This happens to be creative control.

It would be well remarked in the record book
That mind gave priority to oxygen, protein, and fat,
To survive its affinity for blab-blab drive.

Lost today

Hours and hours are growing in my mind.
They altered themselves into a forest
Of unconstructiveness.
A jungle of obstructions facing,
Ostentatiously,
My life.

Yesterday: the tree of the past.

Today: the branches, stretching into perpetual mobile space.

Tomorrow: an insane illusion of making all obstacles
Reversed.

Going nowhere on the way to somewhere

Continuation, consequence, persistence.
This is what one should think.

Here there is no room for perfection,
Because of too-limited time,
To stop within excellence,
And create magnificence.

Too many are held up in the traffic of thoughts;
Too quick are the lights
To pass an existentialist box.

Reflection

In the room of youth,
My maturity is sitting today.
Full of fear, observe—
My tear-soaked eyelashes and lost hope.

This is what I craved.

I dreamed about it, and poured,
Maybe not enough, from the void,
Into a poem,
Full of lightness, frivolity, and joy.

I am because

I am because of the noise of the car.
I am because of the sound of the street.

I am because I'm shouting and calling.
I am because no one hears me.

I am because I look for escape.
I am because I've found it in dreams.

I am because I come back from drowsiness,
And after awakening,
Feel the terrible heaviness of my being.

To my sister

After many years,
I'm older by another
Second of November day.
But it doesn't mean wiser.
I'm still waiting,
Having beside me my husband
Instead of you, my little friend.

It was one of those
Unremembered
Second of November days.
We were standing together
On the hill of unpredictable ways.
It was then that I dared to say,

'Sun come out
Through your cloudy sky,
And brighten, brighten my way!'

Today,
My undistinguished shade
Was willing to say again,
'Sun come out and shine.'
But it didn't dare.

Streetwise

Life divided into two
Creates such a strange design.
Life would like to make its way through,
But it happened
That the door wasn't opened widely enough.

Life got stuck
Between the frame and the handle.
What a decision to make!
To fight the frame?
How stupid!

Better to swing on the handle?

Being upstairs

Science is just about to prove
That there is much more to nothing
Than we had ever thought.

In the heart of nothingness,
Negative energy
Is encouraging the positive to carry on.

Even the lowly zero,
Which made the vicious circle closed,
Is just about to be considered
The greatest figure in algebra—the queen of the science world.

So what about
Affection and feeling
Turned into a void?

While all the built-up energy
Seems to caress
A glass full of wine
Instead of affectionate thoughts.

If I were prettier or younger

If I were prettier or younger,
If I had nothing to lose,
I would have followed you
As a dispossessed soul,
Who had just found her body—
And this body had made her strong.

And then I would become
Your sadness and your happiness,
The platform where your dreams come true,
The scattered ashes of your disappointments,
And the brightest eagle's feather
Enlightening your soul.

It could be and it can be

If poetry could
Rely on the pen I use,
It would still not be so simple.
The pen may inevitably become confused.

By the time I say,
'Calm down!'
The pen would be misplaced again.

Go away—
I would like to mislay you,
And then certainly,
The pen disappeared in a crafty,
Mischievous way.

Come closer—
Who then knows what I wanted to say?
But then,
The pen went through disorder,
And disintegrated into despair.

Relax

Let contentment take over!

Over! *Over!*

Shut up!

I know who it was: I,
Who didn't move any mountains,
Who left the stars where they always were,
Who didn't add anybody to the population.

By definition useless.
Chemistry chose to play a unique trick with me.
I am capable of translating
The language of chemicals
Into damnable confusion,
The rulers of one's life.

I do it.
You choose.
I choose.
You do it.
That's all there is.
I beg your pardon?
Relax!

Let contentment take over!

Things will be going forward
With or without your concerns.
Let contentment take over!

Relax!

Separated

The blue sky of Cracow,
The very Polish and the very old.

The clerk in the booking office
Endlessly could discuss
Which ticket and where to go.

People of the robot era
Make their shadows pass.
And the buildings,
With built-in silent knowledge,
Reflect lapses of time.

The blue sky of Cracow
Protectively looks down,
Taking care of all shadows.
And for the moment, and for a very short time,
Reflects the shadows of you and me.

Jet lag

It's far.
Not far.
Near.
Not near.
In the middle.
Always,
Not always.
Some time any time.
It waves, 'Ciao,'
To sensuality.
Rinses off
Time.
Places itself
Without connection
While playing an effective lullaby.

Blown away

There was a manuscript of short poems,
That was blown away by the wind.
Wind, while blowing, also read the poems,
Very carefully.
And then laughed at them.
Wind couldn't be more mean.

Part Three

From Despair to Hope

The first poems of hope emerging from despair are tainted by the darker colours of the spectrum. But poem by poem, despair is pushed away and hope in her welcome brightness starts to make its presence felt. The dark dame moves away and, one day, is no longer to be seen.

As promised

That which is searched for
Will be found.
What is veiled
Will be revealed.
Chaos
Will become order.

And only Mother Earth-
Indifferent and oblivious,
Failed to deliver the Promised Land
Keeps pirouetting,
As if trying to impress
Some bigger star.

Creation

This is the so-called poem,
Written by a so-called poet,
Sitting at a so-called table,
In the so-called study, except the curtains—yes, curtains.
They were all that was real.

The poet is surrounded by so-called books,
Including those which are about tax avoidance,
And the fulfilment of an impotent hopelessness,
Which actually should be called,
'The phantom of yesterday.'

Or the coagulum of obstacles coagulating against
Evolution, towards tomorrow without change.

Satan's Ball

Ephemeral thoughts are crossing my mind,
That something is wrong, or even very bad.
Will I aim where there is only mist?

Where to dance will invite the Devil arm in arm with the Beast.
Where Satan's symphony will be piercing my senses.

Where the Devil's performance will claim me as I fall to my knees,
Where the Monster's salvation will be saving my sins,
Where the evil of Demons will proclaim me the Queen.

Impression

An impression is coming to me,
In the mist of ancient illusion.
My conscience is flying
Above human goals and their dissolution.

I am there; I am touching the heavens.
My will becomes freedom of mind.
Do you think that it is simple to come back?

And then,

Look into the eyes of mankind?

It was a word at the beginning

When everything seemed to fall short,
Lacking emotion and feeling.
When resignation dressed herself up for us,
With her best proceeding.
When our lack of gentleness,
Was ready to take its toll.
Then unexpectedly came to life—
The Word.

Meaning diversion

Drifting apart in every direction.
'Together.'
Left in every possible way.
'Alone.'

So 'Alone' was strolling today,
Gazing at a closed window.

Behind the window,
A black bird was cawing
In the colour of autumn,
Until something in its voice broke down,
Since 'Alone' with 'Together'
Now walked hand in hand.

Carpe Diem

As it was perpetually said:
Go learn and conquer,
And you will be granted Tomorrow
Without regret.

And Tomorrow will provide
Warmth and the noise of tiny feet playing,
That is heard already.
Go, learn and conquer!

And everything for this Tomorrow—
Everything is dissolving.
Only sometimes I feel sorry for Autumn.
The first leaf fell down, just today.

Jealousy

Suddenly it came to life,
Within a full brain. She,
The brain power you paid respect to,
Dropped me a long way down the competitive ladder.
Flamenco dress; silly poetry.
Please note, poetry can only be silly or profound.
Christian Dior defence.
All crushed.
Note!
I survived.

Letter

Hey! You over there.
Do you remember me?

I walked out on you,
Some memory ago.

Today from the bottom of the wine glass
I presently,
Unpleasantly,
Discharged myself
From the marriage I loved.

And wine, while smoothing sadness down,
Is saying to me:
To Life!

Rerooted

Everything around me seems to be
Stolen from another life.
There must be a reason, why I stop,
Trying to take in:

Different people;
Different holy days and religions;
Different aesthetics and understandings;
Different opportunities and choices;
Different questions and answers;
Different gratitude and appreciation;
Different books in different languages;
Different poems, engrossment in thoughts;
Different arguments and persuasions;
Different.
Different.

It all bears resemblance
To dreams I dreamed a decade ago.
That's why in our sleep,
When we hold hands
In the most indifferent way,
I hold to it.
Like a smile holds to the face.

Appearing,
For many different reasons,
In many different ways.

Where do we come back from?

From a meeting with those whose faces remain young?
From anxiety attempting to give bearing to an uncontrollable line?
From the world of young Hamlet still disturbed by dramatic beliefs?

How strange—how close he is to me.

From behind the curtain,
To the curtain closed behind us?

From the second childhood, then the third, fourth, fifth?
How true it is that the original is nowhere to be seen.

From the multiplicity of colourful flowers in the fields.
From the fragrance.
Oh fragrance, my dimensional king!
Oh fragrance. You, my majesty, my carriage taking me back.
From dimensional life, to the past where I need to return.

From nostalgia.
Step out!

You are entering techno.
You are tough.
You are with money.
You laugh.

Your children have to mix with the proper kind;
Too much responsibility you took.
Do not worry, pretend, smile!

The power of fear

For the purpose of photography
Fear wore a pearl necklace,
Hoping to soften its unmistakable image-
As if it tried to say that as long as there is
The glow of pearls,
There is no need to fear.

For the moment fear got lost
In its self contentedness.

Believing in its own independent being,
It was then summoned to confront the living matters.

And I had to wake up from the fearless dream.

We

We who are always short of sensible words
Step into a minute,
Change seconds into a meaningful world.

We who can't enter. for a while,
Lasting happiness,
Need to comprehend the difference,
Which happens in a split second.

Why have we not been allowed to find the Word?
That which would change uncertainty
Into common day splendour
Or into fairy tale thoughts?

On being armed

You keep saying yes
To the options you are able to hold.
But as long as you do not embrace the impossible,
Limitation is the only target you are aiming for.

So speed your bullet now,
With a vision of mountains and valleys.
Let it be conveyed by your greatest desires.
Burst your neuroses, set fire to bad dreams,

Until the phoenix rises from the ashes
To the regime of discipline.
Let it slow down through excitement,
Speed up through times of calm,

Let miracles be its target
And make a world of it now!

Striving for a poem

Over those blue and blank pages,
A green pen is suspended.

The jazz singer sings beautifully.

And I see, dreamily, my green pen's matter.
Its properties attempting to pierce the vacuum.
Striving to become reality.

Reality raises itself to plausible sensitivity.

And I am in my niche.
Pointlessly exercising cosiness.

Fear after

Oh no! Not today.
I haven't got the strength or the time.
You ask when then?
Oh! Perhaps next year,
Or in a hundred years time?

Are you saying that I might not be alive?
Never mind, come anyway.
You won't be relevant then,
You will be

Fear after life.

Part Four

From Hope to Calm

Does calm come with age or does age come with calm? Does getting older always mean getting wiser? Does getting wiser mean having less anger and more tolerance? Does the asking of questions necessarily lead to plausible answers? No.

I think that the number of questions we pose equals an uncertainty we store up throughout our decades on this earth, growing in parallel with our maturing security and our hope that tomorrow will come and the future may be brightness.

Where there is hope there is calm, and when a poem created in calm and a reader meet, it might result in a subtle, ephemeral journey to the distant place—sometimes as distant as our own, deeply hidden, emotional self.

In the rhythm of the waltz

The next day of my diary
Is the next day of my being.
In a while it will turn itself
Into a dream of dusk,
And then pass by and stop to be.

And a tree?

It roars to the rhythm of the waltz,
Playing staccatos
With its own leaves.

Life counted in years, hours, and seconds;
The hands measure eternal life.

And a tree?

It roars to the rhythm of the waltz
Playing staccatos
With its own leaves.

On the beach

From hand to hand,
I am transferring sand.
It goes through in controllable smaller or larger amounts.

Why should I be upset by offending interactions,
If I relate to the sand?
My playful hands have the capacity to calm me down.

Tranquility

Calm is the ability to earn
A lack of anxiety
And a lack of excitement.

A bird on an apple tree
And another bird-
On another apple tree
Partake in dialogue,
Perhaps concerning justice.

They finished,
But did they reach a conclusion?
Oh! They started again.
Maybe this time the topic is food.

I hope they never stop talking.
While I must remain silent.

The Old Devil Sea

Who are you in front of me?
Able to articulate my name,
But still at a loss
Trying to understand
My unimaginable depth.

A limited caricature.
Undefined.
Two hands and two legs,
Wind blowing her hair
Covering a staring face.

Her motionless surface
Doesn't change at all.
And her depth
Doesn't seem so deep.

Hopefully she might
Bear a grain of my salt on her lips
On the way home.

Landing in Tibet

The snowy peaks were only slightly below.
We flew into them,
Playing in a vast space.
The engines scattered the snow.

We exceeded the expanse,
And found ourselves lost
In the mixture of mountains and clouds.
The plane softly dropped from the nearness of the sky.

The steps we took were short and slow.
Haste belonged now to the other world below.
The earth stopped halfway to heaven.
And here we were subject to a different law.

Breathing constituted its own, ultimate presence;
One had to struggle for …
Breath.
We were creatures from the lower existence,

Elevated and reborn.

The colour of China

The colour red for happiness.
The colour yellow for the kings.
The colour blue for divine,
Dwelling in the round Heaven.
The dark, square Earth
Only was left for me.

I felt free to walk
Into the Red Glory.
To breathe deeply of the colour of my dreams.
I walk further—stepping into Yellow.
I become Empress.
I rule over the colours,
Order them to stay still.
They rebel!
Change their hue every hour,
Of every season, month and day.

Despairing I slipped into Blue—
I feel safe.
Guided by spheres.
I am the circle,
The middle.
The goodness.

And an unbalanced badness.

Stranger

Not to know you
Doesn't worry me so much.
You manage to vibrate the unyielding membrane.
Unpredictably arranged.

Unpredictably different.
Differently unattached.
You may disturb the forgotten,
Woman's maternal touch.

Everlasting summer

There is a space between us.
It is filled with hot air.
There is the Saigon River.
Bats flying above.
Unfamiliar reasons for laughing,
As if we had lost the common touch.

It might as well be another planet,
With common time,
Or uncommon enough,
To make us weightless.

And able to fly.

A drop of adjustment

One cold drop of rain,
On my naked arm,
Woke me up to hot Saigon.
To the hands of a smart watch,
That had faded and stopped turning.

As if time had changed its recognition,
Direction, understanding, and span.
And progressed in parallel lines,
From the clock face to infinity
Without years, days or months.

Back to idyll

The tropical beach.

You, *the sea,* and I.
Nothing has changed.
As if we all, and the starlight,
Travelling for millions of years to reach us,
Have never been apart.

The waves are chanting
Nursery rhymes to the sleepless night.
The same will be heard here timelessly;
But our sleep
Will soon break
With the first ray of light.

Victoria's frogs

My family and I lived a luxurious life,
Within the sea-view pond.
A garden of paradise was ours.
We sang the happy song all day and all night,
Until disaster came,
With tons of sand.
My family and I were lucky
To survive.

The frog dynasty
Got scattered—some here, some on the other side.
Sometimes I sit under the bush and miss the time
When we, all together,
Sang.

Good luck from Angkor

The motionless dance
Of the silent stones.
The Apsara
Will step very soon out of the wall.

The meditating figures,
Who sit proudly and rigidly,
Side by side on the wall,
Very shortly will be cleared
Of all illusions and will find freedom,
Outside their boundaries.

And the elephants,
In a minute or so,
Will form into a circle,
With their trunks rising up to the sky,
And trumpeting,
To proclaim a new century.
A new time.

And all the royals
On the Terrace of the Kings,
Will take their seats,
And together proclaim
A long awaited peace.

Lotus flowers engraved in the rigid stone—
They will grow, disobeying the order of entropy,
To become a beautiful carpet,
Spreading out from every wall,
Such that nobody will ever know which is a flower
And which is a stone.

Balcony

This is our balcony.
And within the distance of touch
The neighbouring one,
Containing vivid vegetation, the Orchid, etc.

There is also resident- the Lady Buddha,
And seen as a patch of sky
At the base of that arrangement
Is a pool of water.

Space glances at limitation and laughs.
My thought is-
It looks like I went through.

The desert garden

It is difficult to remember
Why a sand pit was such fun—
A square of happiness.
The deeper I dig, the happier I become.

I dig in the sand again,
Pouring upon it unnumbered water cans.
How much digging my garden spade should take,
To bring back innocent memory?
To grow into the garden of pride?

Something is saying in me,
Sand is only sand.
Nothing really can grow on it,
Except poorly-looking plants.

It took millennia for sand to become
Formed from the stones' harshness,
To escape rigidity and hardness.
Why would suddenly the sand be accommodating?
Embracing the plants?

Isn't nothingness
The ultimate goal of sand?

Justification

Now, when the whole world stands still.
I can relieve myself of dependency,
Of the relativity of time,

Of the lightness of wellbeing,
Of excitement and stagnation,
Of an absurd question:
To move or to stay still?

All answers, doubts and questions,
Go indefinitely around.
And suddenly became motionless in the shape
Of a big
?

All persuasion, confidence and affection,
Also stayed put,
Within the border of an
!

Exclamation and Question.
An incompatible team,
They stopped for a moment,
To justify
An unanswerable
To be.

Calmness

Being here
Means to forget about variety.
Rather surrendering to a pushy reality,
To cosiness.

More like thinking, thoughtlessly.
Dreaming, dreamlessly.
Coming and going.
But unconsciously.

From the time arranged, to be back.
To switching off, maybe wrongly, relativity theory.

Tradition

We are in the morning,
And in the evening.
Day by day ordinary,
But sometimes a shadow of legend,
Or a trial of metamorphosis.

Imperfect imagination of a different life,
The ring of the bells,
Mourning loss,
Or the winning fanfare.
The sound of analysis and synthesis.
Important papers,
Signed by loving or hating hands.

Sometimes interior trembling

Annual repetition.
Happy tears.
Nostalgic smiles.

Be careful to add to it with dignity
And never let it ...die.

To be born now or later

I see you.
You are active.
Although a world of thin skin separates us,
I put my hand to feel you.

You stopped doing what you were doing,
And listened- your energy got lower,
Your heartbeat slowed,
As if you were having doubts.

Which I don't mind.

And when you cross your boundary and we meet at last.
It will be like the sound of the jungle,
Like the tropical rain falling,
Like the sun setting over the desert
Like facing Quoma-Langma.
The holy mountain.

Feeling so small and so grateful that you arrived
Can you feel yet my excitement?
Can you feel it now?
Enter this world when you are ready,
And let excitement carry you to my arms.

Dirty hands
(Philosophically speaking)

And nobody can own
An action.
Morally responsible, and
Sleepless for tonight.
The sun stops
On some boring guy's head.

Putting emphasis on choices.

That dilemma reveals to you
What you behold.
I let myself off the hook,
Which led me to a utilitarian view.
And so I shot the Indian instead.

To guarantee the ethical choices
Is uneasy.
And the way to do it
Is to chop the head off
And not to commit treason.

Meantime the sun left the
boring guy's head.

And no further questions.

I love you my way

The Day

In the morning
I love you like a sea breeze that refreshes perception and makes
the horizon clear.

For breakfast
My love spreads so that you can choose anything that is healthy,
tasty and fresh, like squeezed orange juice.

For the working hours
I love you like a hundred tasks to be performed and which have
to be done.
If they all proceed smoothly, then my love is happy and bright.
But when love feels overwhelmed it gets angry and bites.

For the homecoming time
Love listens for the sound of your car.

For dinner
My love tastes like a sip of wine, that complements whatever
you choose to have.

At the time when soft music plays
My love soothes, restores straightness, relaxes and moderates.

Sometimes, when the music gets loud
My love feels like a dancer, and does what dancers do: spins around.

At the time of intimacy
My love rolls into a cocoon, and inside are we alone.
The outside loses significance, and the only thing that counts is
silky touch.

In the starry night

My love is like starlight travelling for millions of years to arrive and enrich you with infinity, to give you a universe that expands.

The Seasons

As for spring,

My love dresses in different colours, from lilac through green to the bright yellow of the sun, to make you feel the diversity of life.

In the Summer

I love you like a hot sunny day: my warmth caresses and relaxes, and feels safe.

In the Autumn

I love you in brown.
I let fall the leaves to add softness to walk on the ground.

Come the Winter

My love emanates heat that for you is warming just to look at me.

The Changes

At the time of nightmare

In which you want to leave, my love becomes a fear, and wakes up in terror as if you were the air I need to breathe.

At the stormy time

My love subdues.
The elements fight, until a ray of sun appears and makes love again arise.

At the time of moving

From place to place, my love becomes a carrier to take half of your heaviness.

At the time of panic
When we get slightly mad, my love stretches time, and
  accommodates your concerns.

In challenging times,
My love becomes the wall of achievement, unmoving, proud,
  silent, reflecting what you have achieved.

At the time when we need to part
My love becomes the magnetic field that pulls you close,
  regardless of how far you might be.

Printed in the United States
by Baker & Taylor Publisher Services